**W9-AWJ-915**

Eager Street Academy #884
401 East Eager Street
Baltimore, MD 21202

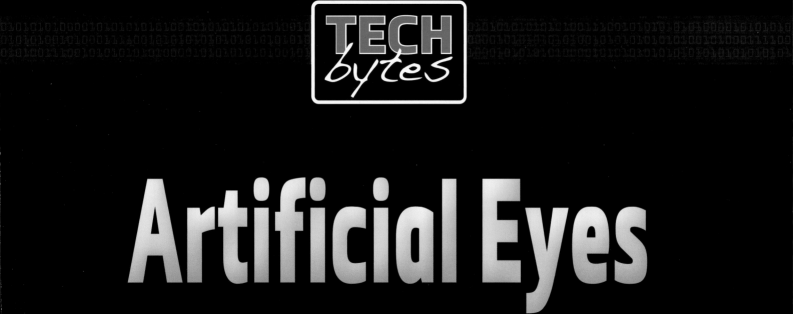

# Artificial Eyes

Cover: A person places a contact lens on an artificial eye.

Norwood House Press
P.O. Box 316598
Chicago, Illinois 60631

For information regarding Norwood House Press, please visit our website at:
www.norwoodhousepress.com or call 866-565-2900.

**LIBRARY OF CONGRESS CATALOGING-IN-PUBLICATION DATA**

Sheen, Barbara, author.
 Artificial eyes / by Barbara Sheen.
      pages cm -- (Tech bytes)
 Audience: Ages 8-12.
 Audience: Grades 4 to 6.
 Summary: "Describes the invention and development of Artificial Eyes. Explores trials and tribulations along with the technological advances seen today. Includes glossary, websites, and bibliography for further reading"-- Provided by publisher.
 Includes bibliographical references and index.
 ISBN 978-1-59953-761-0 (library edition : alk. paper) -- ISBN 978-1-60357-874-5 (ebook)
 1.  Eyes, Artificial--Juvenile literature. 2.  Medical technology--Juvenile literature. 3.  Medical innovations--Juvenile literature. 4. Vision--Juvenile literature.  I. Title.
 RE986.S54 2016
 617.7'9--dc23
                                                              2015027486

289N—062016
Manufactured in the United States of America in Brainerd, Minnesota.

# CONTENTS

Note: Words that are **bolded** in the text are defined in the glossary.

# CHAPTER 1

# An Evolving Idea

Teddy looks like any other little boy, but Teddy has something that most other kids do not have. He has an **ocular prosthesis**, or artificial eye. When Teddy was two years old, he was diagnosed with a rare form of cancer in his eye. To rid him of the disease, his eye was surgically removed. Then Teddy was fitted with a custom-made artificial eye. To make sure that it fit right, the eye was molded to fit into Teddy's **eye socket**. The color was carefully matched to Teddy's other eye. When Teddy looks around, the eye moves. Teddy can cry real tears with both his eyes, too. The only thing Teddy's artificial eye cannot do is restore his vision.

Even though Teddy cannot see out of his artificial eye, it helps in other ways. If a child's eye is missing, the bones around the eye may not grow right. Teddy's custom-fitted eye helps support the growth of the eye socket and the bones in his face. Also, without the support of an eye, a person's eyelid shrinks and sags and the eyelid loses its ability to open, close, or blink away things like dust and pollen. Teddy's artificial eye helps his eyelid work right. It looks so real that it is hard to tell Teddy's eyes apart.

## Replacing an Eye

Eyes do more than let people see. They also show emotion and give social cues. A person's eyes are one of the first things

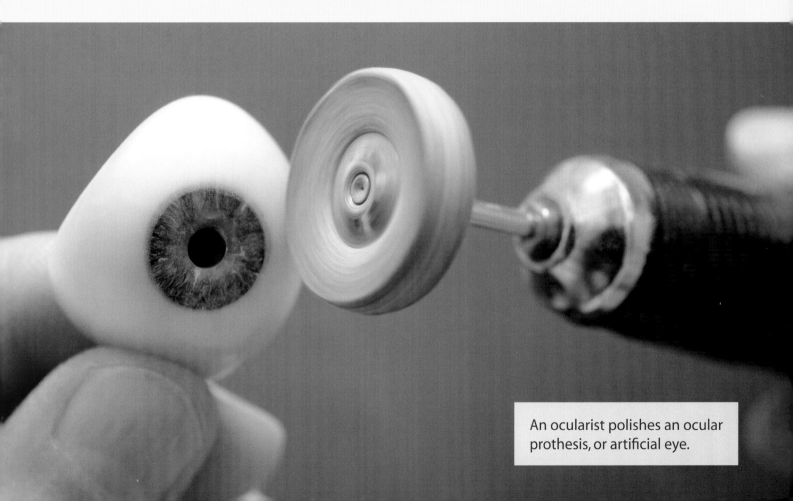

An ocularist polishes an ocular prothesis, or artificial eye.

others notice. Humans have been making artificial or "fake" eyes for centuries, but inventors had to solve many problems before an eye like Teddy's could be made.

One problem was figuring out how to keep a fake eye in the eye socket. Another was finding the right material for the eye. Some materials irritated the eye socket.

Some were too fragile. Others absorbed moisture and caused the fake eye to be covered with mucus. Inventors thought about ways to fill the eye socket so that the eyelid would not sag and the tissue around the missing eye would grow right. They worried over how to customize the fit and they thought about how to make the fake eye move in sync with the other eye. It took hundreds of years and many people to create the realistic fake eyes that are used today.

## Ancient Eyes

Ancient Egyptians, Greeks, and Romans all made artificial eyes. These eyes were quite different than modern eyes. In fact, they were clearly fake. Early artificial eye makers did not know how to form a fake eye that fit under the eyelid. Instead, fake eyes were worn over the eyelid like a patch. They were made of clay and painted to look like an eye. The eyes were fastened to a piece of cloth and held in place over the eyelid with some form of adhesive. These early eyes did not look real at all, but they kept dirt out of the eye socket and they were less disturbing to onlookers than an empty eye socket.

## Under the Eyelid

Artificial eyes were worn on top of the eyelid until the late 16th century. Then a French surgeon named Ambroise Paré thought of placing a fake eye made of gold beneath the eyelid of a patient. Soon

## Special Eyes

Most ancient fake eyes were made of clay, but fake eyes for the rich helped show their status. They were made of gold, silver, and crystal. Special fake eyes made of gold, silver, crystal, and bronze were also made for the dead. These eyes were often placed in the tombs of Egyptian mummies. The Egyptians believed that the eyes gave the dead everlasting vision and helped guide them into the next world. The ancient Romans made fake eyes out of precious metals, too. These eyes were not for the living or the dead. Instead, they were placed in the eye sockets of statues.

In the late 16th century a French surgeon named Ambroise Paré recommended placing a fake eye made of gold beneath the eyelid of a patient.

craftspersons were making gold, silver, and glass eyes that could be worn under the eyelid. These eyes were U-shaped and very thin. They were made in only one size and did not fit everyone. Unfortunately, they did not have enough volume to keep the eyelid from drooping, and had other problems as well. The eyes had sharp edges. These scratched the wearer's eye socket and led to infections, however, they looked better than the ancient fake eyes.

## Glass Eyes

Little changed until the late 19th century. Then an eye surgeon named Hermann Snellen used a new type of lightweight glass to make a

# Golden Eye

In 2006 archaeologists found a skeleton on the Irani-Afghan border. It belonged to a 5,000-year-old female. Buried with the skeleton was a fake eye. Experts say that the eye may have been worn under the owner's eyelid. This makes it unique. The eye was made of an oily paste and covered with a layer of gold. It was engraved with a central circle. This was adorned with golden sun-like rays. The wearer was believed to be a high priestess. Experts say that the eye was thought to give the wearer magical powers.

thicker fake eye. This eye had rounded edges. The rounded edges made it more comfortable and less dangerous than earlier eyes. The design was very popular. Soon glassblowers were making hundreds of these eyes. They used different colors of glass to imitate the colors of a real eye, but they kept the exact process a secret. Germany became the center of the artificial eye

## DID YOU KNOW? ?

To make early glass eyes, a tube of glass was heated at one end until a molten ball formed. Glassblowers used their skills to form the ball into a fake eye.

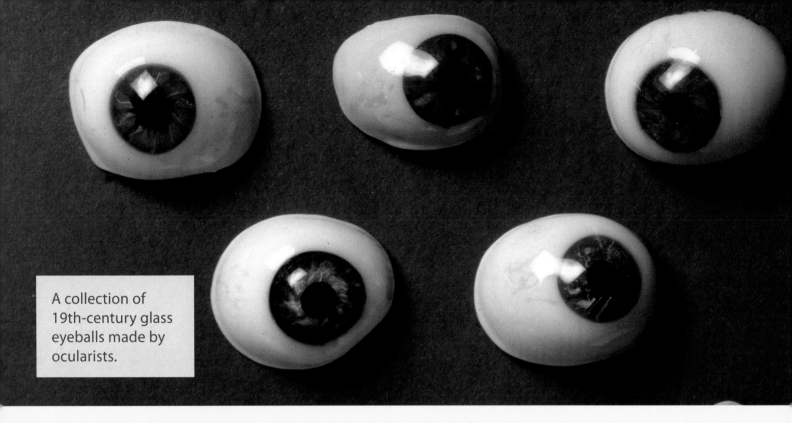

A collection of 19th-century glass eyeballs made by ocularists.

industry. The glassblowers who made the eyes became known as **ocularists**.

People could order the eyes through the mail or they could go to optical shops and browse through trays filled with glass eyes. Shops kept a large number of the eyes in stock, therefore they became known as stock eyes. These eyes were very popular, but they were far from perfect. They did not have enough volume to support the eyelid very well. They also shattered easily. Plus, because glass is porous, the eyes absorbed eye liquids like tears and mucus and had to be cleaned often. Since the eye did not move like a real eye, it did not look natural.

## The Orbital Implant

In 1841 an English surgeon named Phillip Henry Mules sought to make stock eyes look more real. He did this by implanting a glass sphere known as an **orbital implant** into the eye socket of a patient who had lost an eye. The device is about the size of a Ping-Pong ball. It gave fake eyes something to rest on. It also provided the volume needed to lessen eyelid droop. Mules hoped that the muscles in the back of the eye socket that move a real eye would move the implant. He thought this would also move the fake eye that

## Exploding Eyes

Glass eyes have been known to explode. The glass for the eyes was not always heated or cooled enough when the eyes were being made. This meant the eyes were very brittle. Sudden changes in temperature caused the glass to contract or expand. The brittle glass could not stand the change in pressure, so it shattered. Usually this happened in the manufacturer's cases, but medical records from 1918 state that 18 fake eyes shattered while in people's eye sockets.

## DID YOU KNOW?

The town of Lauscha, Germany, was once famous for making the best glass eyes in the world. Artisans in Lauscha began working with glass to make doll eyes. They used the same skills to create artificial eyes.

1989 experts made an orbital implant from a mineral found in ocean coral. This mineral is very similar to human bone so the body accepts it. Because the patient's blood vessels grow into it, the eye muscles can be attached directly to it. This makes it possible for the fake eye that sits on the outside of the implant to move just like a real eye.

## Custom-Fitted Plastic Eyes

Even with an orbital implant in place, glass eyes were less than ideal. Also, during World War II, there was a shortage of German glass eyes. This caused inventors to try other materials. The American military wanted to give soldiers who had lost eyes artificial ones, so it began to try out plastic. Dentists

rested on the implant, but the muscles could not be attached to the glass implant. Unfortunately, eye movement could not be restored and implants were often rejected by the wearer's immune system.

For the next century experts tried to create a better orbital implant. They tried a lot of different substances. In

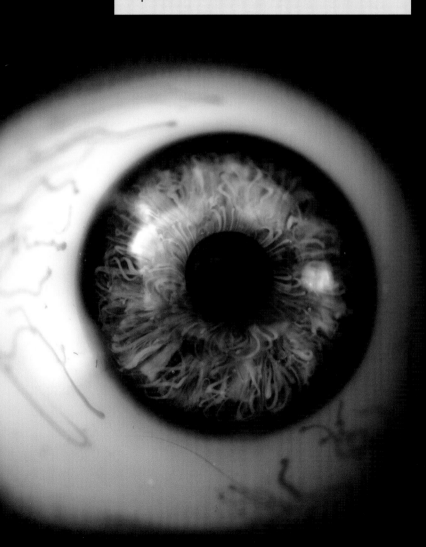

A close up view of an orbital implant with a prosthesis shows its realistic details.

were already using a clear acrylic plastic to make the base of dentures. It was called polymethyl methacrylate (PMMA). A group of military dental technicians figured out how to compress PMMA. This meant it could be used to make fake eyes.

Plastic eyes turned out to be much better than glass eyes. They were stronger. They lasted longer. They also did not absorb eye fluid. This meant tears could flow over them, and they did not need to be removed and cleaned as often. Plastic is also more flexible than glass and is easier to shape

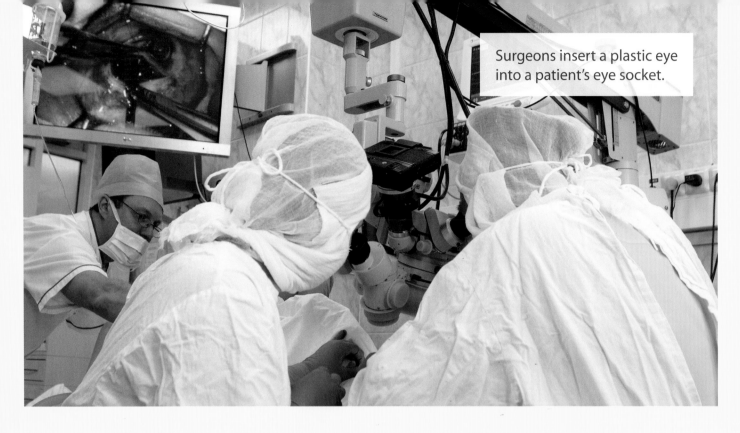

Surgeons insert a plastic eye into a patient's eye socket.

than glass. In 1969 American ocularists Lee Allen and Howard Webster found a way to take an impression (much like a dental impression) of the eye socket. This was used to custom-make plastic eyes that fit the contours of a person's eye socket perfectly. Plastic eyes could be painted to match the other eye, too. After thousands of years and many innovations, by the end of the 20th century people who lost an eye could finally have a fake eye that looked realistic.

# CHAPTER 2

# A Multistep Procedure

It takes the work of many professionals to replace a diseased or damaged eye. Doing so is a multistep procedure. It is both science and art. Learning about the structure of the eye and how it works makes it easier to understand the process.

## The Eye

The eye consists of many parts that work with the brain to let people see. The eye sits behind the eyelid in the eye socket. Six muscles that move the eye attach to the eye in the back of the eye socket. The eyelid protects the eye by blinking.

When someone blinks, a tiny bit of fluid known as tears is released from the upper part of the eyelid. Tears wash away foreign objects and keep the eye from drying out. The white part of the eye is the **sclera**. It is the eye's protective outer coat. Tiny red lines that pass through it are blood vessels. The **cornea** is also found on the outer part of the eye. It helps focus incoming light. Behind the cornea is a colored ring called the **iris**. The iris has a circular opening called the **pupil**. The **retina** is a nerve layer that lines the back of the eye.

# Human Eye Anatomy

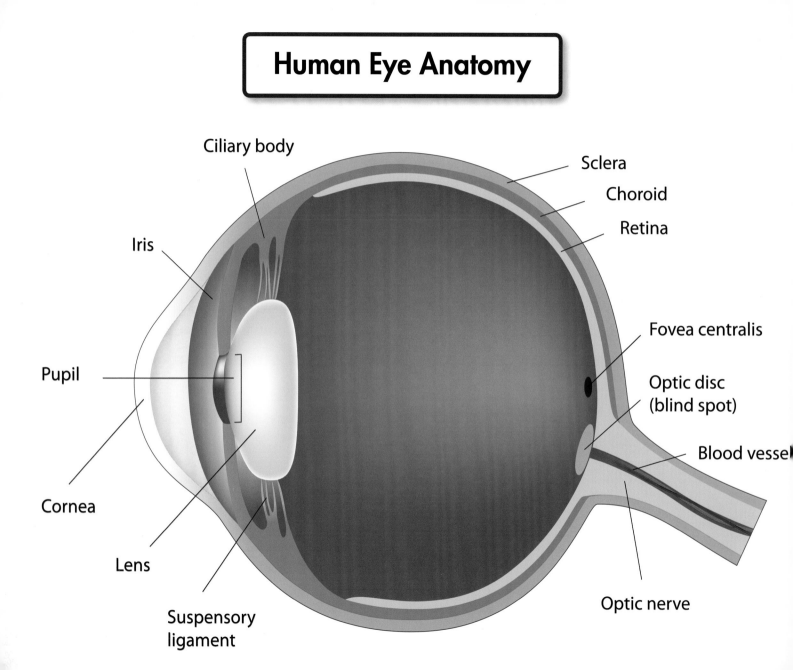

Ciliary body

Iris

Pupil

Cornea

Lens

Suspensory
ligament

Sclera

Choroid

Retina

Fovea centralis

Optic disc
(blind spot)

Blood vessel

Optic nerve

# Eye Surgery

The first step in replacing an eye is the removal of all or part of a diseased or damaged eye. The surgery is done in a hospital by an **ophthalmologist**, or eye surgeon. First, patients are put to sleep so they are unconscious during the procedure. There are two types of surgeries. In the first type the whole eye is removed. For this to happen, the **optic nerve** must be severed. In the second type most of the eye is removed, but the optic nerve is left intact. If the whole eye has been removed, an orbital implant is placed in the eye socket. The muscles that move the eye are attached to the implant. This will allow the fake eye to move in a natural way. Until a fake eye can be worn, a temporary device called a conformer shell is placed on top

An ophthalmologist performs eye replacement surgery.

of the implant or on top of what is left of the real eye. It looks like a large contact lens. By filling the empty space, it helps keep the eye cavity from shrinking and the eyelid functioning. Finally, the doctor puts a patch over the eye. It protects the eye socket and keeps the eyelid closed.

Patients wear the patch for about five days. Once the patch is removed, patients are given a healing gel to apply to their eye socket. This is not painful. Patients are often surprised to see that their eye socket does not look like an empty hole. Muscle and tissues make it look pink.

## Making an Impression

About six weeks after surgery, work on the fake eye can begin. First the ocularist

# Eye-Care Professionals

There are a variety of jobs for people who want to work in eye care. Ophthalmologists are medical doctors. They focus on eye care. They can do surgery and they can prescribe medicine. Optometrists are not medical doctors. They do vision exams. They prescribe glasses and contact lenses. They detect eye defects. They can also prescribe medicine for some eye diseases. Opticians are not doctors. They are trained to fit glasses. They follow prescriptions from ophthalmologists and optometrists. They do not test vision or dispense medicine. An ocularist is a specialist who fits and makes fake eyes.

makes an impression of the front part of the patient's eye socket where the fake eye will go. To do this, the oculist inserts a needleless syringe into a patient's eye socket and injects a special cream. Patients say this feels strange but does not hurt.

In about a minute, the cream hardens to the consistency of the white of a hard-boiled egg. Then the impression is removed from the eye socket. A two-sided **plaster of Paris** mold is made around the impression. Hot wax is poured into the hardened mold. A plastic button is cut to the exact size of the patient's natural iris. This is pressed into the center of the wax mold. Once the wax cools, it becomes the model for the fake eye.

An ocularist inserts and removes the wax model from the patient's eye socket until it fits perfectly atop the orbital implant.

# Becoming an Ocularist

Ocularists fit and make fake eyes. They also show patients how to handle and care for these eyes. There are no schools that train them. Instead, they must serve as an apprentice. They work under a board certified ocularist. This lasts five years. They must also take 750 hours of study courses. These courses are offered by the American Society of Ocularists. This is a group that certifies ocularists. After a person serves as an apprentice and does the coursework, he or she can be certified as an ocularist.

The fake eye must fit right. So the ocularist inserts and removes the wax model from the patient's eye socket many times. Each time the model is removed, the ocularist alters its shape. This is done until the eye fits comfortably on top of the orbital implant, allows the eyelid to work normally, and looks real. This is a hard task. It takes the skill of a sculptor.

## From a Wax Model to an Eye

Next the wax model is made into a fake eye. To make this happen, a plaster of Paris mold is made from the wax model. Then dough made of PMMA is packed into the plaster of Paris mold. The plastic iris button is inserted into the dough. The dough is heated until a plastic duplicate of the mold forms. This becomes the fake eye. It is designed to fit over the orbital implant and fill the front of the eye socket,

An ocularist paints an artificial eye.

so it is not round like a real eye. Instead, it is U-shaped. In order to make the eye look real, it must be painted. To ensure it matches the patient's real eye, the ocularist studies the patient's iris, pupil, and sclera. Then, using oil paint and a tiny brush, the ocularist sets to work. First the iris button is painted. An iris is not one color. It is a blend of many colors. So duplicating it requires the work of an artist. The sclera,

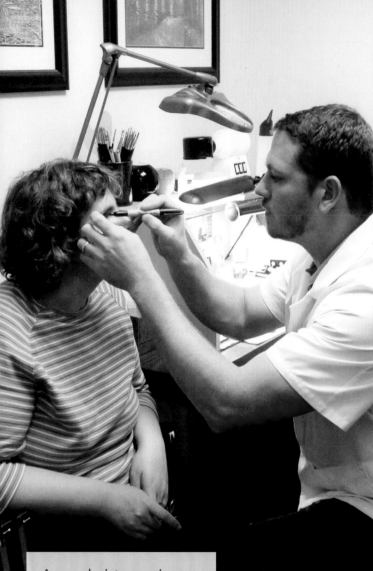

An ocularist examines an ocular prosthesis on a patient.

too, is not one shade of white. Plus, it has tiny red blood vessels that run through it. The ocularist paints these on with silk thread. Time and again, the fake eye is placed in the patient's eye socket and removed so the coloring can be modified. Once the color is perfect, the eye is put back in the plaster mold and covered with a layer of clear plastic that is heated until it hardens. This protects the color. Finally, the eye is polished to a high gloss and fitted under the patient's eyelid.

## Artificial Eye Maintenance

Unlike old-fashioned fake eyes, a custom-made plastic eye needs little care. In fact, the less a person handles the eye, the better. This helps avoid infections. People sleep with the eye in place. They remove the

# Painting an Iris

Most ocularists use a patient's real eye as a model for the color of the fake eye. This means that the patient must be there while the fake eye is being painted. Patients would not have to be there if photos were used instead. The ocularist could take photos of the patient's real eye with a digital camera. Then they could print the photos and paint from them. Most prefer not to do this. The reason is that the color of the eye changes slightly with different lighting. Depending on the light and the angle of the photos, the eye color would appear slightly different in each one. When the photos are printed, the type of printer and the inks used can also cause the eye color to be slightly off.

eye once every few weeks to clean it with water or contact lens cleaning solution. Removing the eye is not hard. It is done in much the same way as a contact lens is removed.

About once a year the ocularist polishes the eye. This makes the eye look brighter and more natural. During this visit, the ocularist checks the eye's fit and the health of the eye socket. The tissue around the eye socket changes over time, so fake eyes need to be replaced every three to five years. They must be replaced more often in kids who outgrow their eyes. Whether a fake eye is made for an adult or a child, it is clear that the process is complex. It takes knowledge of the eye and artistic talent. The final product is well worth the effort.

# CHAPTER 3

# Changing Lives

Peter was in the US Army. In 2003 a car bomb blew up in Tal Afar, Iraq. Peter was hit with sharp metal pieces from the exploding car. He had severe injuries that left him blind in one eye. Two other members of Peter's platoon also were blinded in one eye by the blast. Severe eye injuries are common in wars. Thirteen percent of all troops wounded in Iraq or Afghanistan have had surgery for eye wounds, and 142 of these service members were blinded in one eye as result of blast injuries.

War is not the only cause of eye loss. The American Society to Prevent Blindness says that 10,000 to 12,000 Americans lose an eye each year. About 50 percent of these eye losses are caused by accidents. Disease is another big cause of eye loss. Some babies are born with a rare form of cancer. It is known as retinoblastoma. In this type of cancer a tumor forms in the eye. About 70 percent of kids in the United States with this cancer have eye removal surgery. This is about 300 kids per year. There are other diseases that may

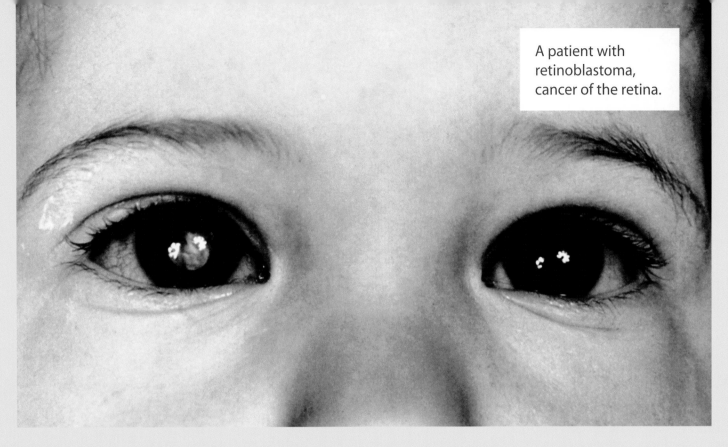

A patient with retinoblastoma, cancer of the retina.

result in the removal of an eye. These are more likely to strike adults. They include eye diseases like glaucoma and cataracts. They also include diseases like diabetes, which can affect the eyes.

## Emotional Issues

No matter what causes a person to lose an eye, eye loss takes a big toll on people. The eyes are a key part of a person's face. Their color, size, and shape help define a person's looks, and people's eyes often show their feelings. People are often judged by what their eyes "say." Studies have found that people who make eye contact with others are seen as more attractive than people who do not make eye contact. They are also seen as more likeable and honest. There are many common eye-related sayings. These show how people judge others by what they see in their eyes. For instance, the eyes are often called the windows to the soul. Dishonest people are often described as having shifty eyes. Cruel people are sometimes described as being dead behind the eyes. Attractive people are often said to have sparkling or twinkling eyes.

It should come as no surprise that many people who have lost an eye report feeling depressed, anxious, and self-conscious. They worry about their looks and about how others may react to them. As a result, they may isolate themselves. They may avoid social activities or contact with others.

Kids and teens who lose an eye, especially, feel uncomfortable. They are often teased by other kids because of their

Eyes are very important to the way a person looks.

looks. The longer a child goes without a fake eye, the more likely that he or she will start to look disfigured. This is because as kids grow, so does the tissue around the eyes. Without a fake eye, the tissue around the missing eye may not grow at the same pace as that of the other eye. This makes the person's face look lopsided. This often makes the teasing worse. Some kids who lose an eye get into trouble trying to defend themselves. Others become shy and withdrawn.

## Getting an Artificial Eye Makes a Difference

For many people, getting a fake eye changes their life. It restores their confidence and feelings of self-worth. It makes them feel more secure around other people and it makes others feel more at ease interacting

# Eye Protection

Many accidents can cause eye loss, but people can take steps to protect their eyes. They can wear goggles in places where chemicals or debris can go flying. This includes building sites, science labs, and metal and wood shops. Goggles or other eyewear also protect eyes from injury during sports such as tennis, hockey, and football. They also protect the eyes of motorcyclists.

Infections can also lead to eye loss. People can help ward these off. They can shake off dust and debris from goggles before taking them off. Not rubbing the eyes with dirty hands or a dirty cloth also helps prevent infection. So does washing the hands before touching the eye area.

with them. The change can be quite dramatic. This was the case with a woman whose grandchild was hesitant to come near her after the woman lost her eye. The woman worried that because of the way she looked, she and the child would never be close again, but once the woman got a fake eye, everything changed. When the little girl first saw her grandmother with her fake eye, she jumped into the woman's arms and hugged her. At that moment, the woman felt that her life was back to normal.

Other people say that getting a fake eye helped them get their life back on track, too. They say that having an artificial eye makes them feel normal. In fact, they say that most people cannot tell which of their eyes is real and which is not so they are treated just like everyone else and are not judged unfairly.

## Helping the Poor

Most Americans who suffer an eye loss have access to fake eyes. This is not the case for people in many developing nations. In some countries people do not have much access to medical care. This is especially true for poor people in rural villages. Even in some large cities, there are few trained ocularists, or there may not be any. People may have to travel to Europe or North America to get a custom-made fake eye. Even if they can get a custom-made eye locally, it is often too costly for the poor to afford.

A number of charitable medical groups are working to help these people. These groups send volunteers that include doctors and ocularists to villages throughout the

This eye clinic in western Ethiopia was built in 2007 by a British charity.

# Eye Loss and Sports

People who lose an eye must adjust to many things. One of these is that the loss of an eye reduces their depth and distance perception. This affects many aspects of a person's life. For those who play sports, limited depth and distance perception makes it hard to judge the position of a moving ball. This makes sports like football, tennis, and baseball very hard. With practice, people can adjust to this new perception and continue to play sports. In fact, having one eye can actually help people in sports like shooting and archery. People with one eye do not have to close an eye to line up the target.

world. The volunteers set up temporary clinics. There they provide local people with all types of eye care. Patients travel for hours to get to the clinics. Much of the care involves giving eye tests and dispensing glasses. Some of these patients have lost an eye due to disease or violence in their nation. Most do not have a fake eye. As a result of having an empty eye socket for a long time, their eyelid droops and the affected side of their face looks crooked.

To help these people, the doctors do surgery to repair sagging eyelids and facial tissue when needed, and the ocularists fit the patients with fake eyes. About 20 to 50 eyes are dispensed each year by these clinics. One case was a

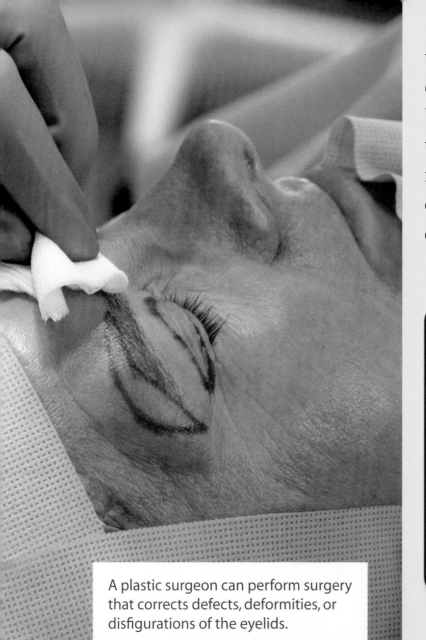

A plastic surgeon can perform surgery that corrects defects, deformities, or disfigurations of the eyelids.

teenage girl who had a deformed, blind eye. The doctors removed the eye. Upon the medical group's next visit, the ocularist fitted the girl with a well-made fake eye. Having the eye greatly changed her looks and improved the quality of her life.

## DID YOU KNOW? ?

**Some people have special designs painted onto their fake eyes. These include tiny team logo "tattoos" that are painted onto the white of the artificial eye. One man has an artificial eye with a happy face instead of an iris.**

## Helping War Victims

Other charitable groups focus on helping kids who have lost an eye due to war. Just as US service members have had serious eye injuries in Afghanistan and Iraq, so have many kids in these nations. These groups bring injured kids to the United States to receive medical care

A charity brought Shah Bibi to the United States where she was fitted with a prosthetic arm, and a custom-made artificial eye.

# Making Misaligned Eyes Look Normal

Some people are born with a misaligned or crossed eye. The condition affects a person's looks and often lowers the person's self-esteem. The eye can be made to look normal with a scleral shell. This is a thin shell, similar to a thick contact lens. It is designed to fit over an existing eye and made to look exactly like the patient's other eye. Scleral shells, which work like a contact lens, can be made so that patients see through them. This lets people with misaligned eyes that can still see, improve their looks without limiting their vision.

and custom-fitted fake eyes. Shah Bibi is one of these kids. She picked up a shiny object on the side of the road near her home in Afghanistan. It was a discarded live grenade. It exploded and left Shah Bibi without a right arm and right eye. The Children of War Foundation is a medical charity. It brought Shah Bibi to the United States for treatment. The little girl was fitted with a prosthetic arm and a custom-made fake eye. Shah Bibi's new eye cannot restore her vision, but it makes her look and feel normal. This has changed the girl's life for the better.

# CHAPTER 4

# What the Future Holds

Many people are working on projects that involve artificial eyes and vision. Some work to improve the looks of fake eyes. They also work to make fake eyes more accessible. Others work to create a **bionic eye**. This is an eye that can restore vision.

## A Working Pupil

Modern fake eyes look real, but there are a lot of differences between them. One big difference is the way the pupil in a real eye responds to changes in light. When a real eye is exposed to bright light, the pupil contracts. In low light, the pupil enlarges. The pupil in a fake eye does not change in different light conditions. As a result, it does not look completely life-like.

Experts at Nottingham Trent University in England are working to change this. They are working on a fake eye with a pupil that responds to light. The pupil of the eye is made of carbon paste and smart material. Carbon paste is a substance that electrodes can pass through. Smart

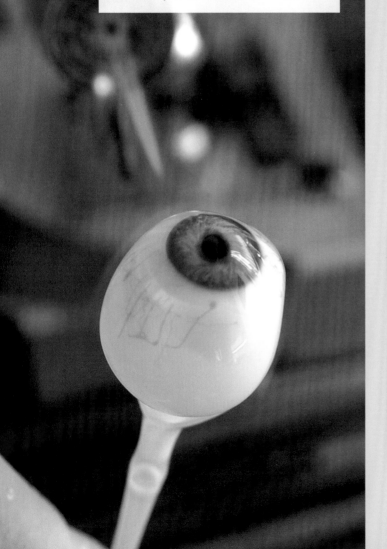

Scientists in England developed an artificial eye that lets in light. The pupil of the eye is made of carbon paste and smart material.

material responds to an electric current. It will change its shape or color.

This pupil has a light sensor in it. The sensor is powered by a small battery. When the sensor detects a change in light, it "talks" with a computer program or controller. This is built into the artificial eye. The controller decides how much power the pupil needs to be the right size

## DID YOU KNOW? ?

**The cost of a custom-made artificial eye ranges from about $2,000 to $8,000. Health insurance typically pays for an artificial eye for those people who need one.**

# Bionics

Bionics is a fairly new field of science. It replaces or improves body parts. Bionic body parts differ from other artificial body parts like eyes. This is because they closely copy the function of the body part they replace. Some may even improve on it. A cochlear implant restores hearing to some deaf people. It not only helps people hear, it filters out background noises better than some real ears.

based on the amount of light the sensor detects. It then sends an electric charge to the pupil. When the pupil gets the charge, it expands or contracts the right amount. Experts are working to perfect the device.

## 3-D Printed Eyes

Another group is looking at a different issue. Getting a fake eye is a problem for many people in the world. They may not have enough money for the eye. Or they may lack access to fake eyes. Experts at Fripp Design and Research in England hope to solve this problem. They are using a 3-D printer to mass-produce affordable fake eyes. 3-D printers can create solid objects from a digital model. To make the eyes, an image of an eye is digitally created. This is done with computer-aided design software. The digital model is sent to the printer. The printer reproduces the model in three dimensions. It does this by laying down layers of powdered material until an artificial eye is formed.

The eyes are held together with resin. This is a sticky natural substance. The eyes are made in large batches. They come in three sizes. The iris color in each batch is slightly different. This makes it possible to closely match a person's real eye. About 150 fake eyes can be made in an hour. The cost is about 97 percent less

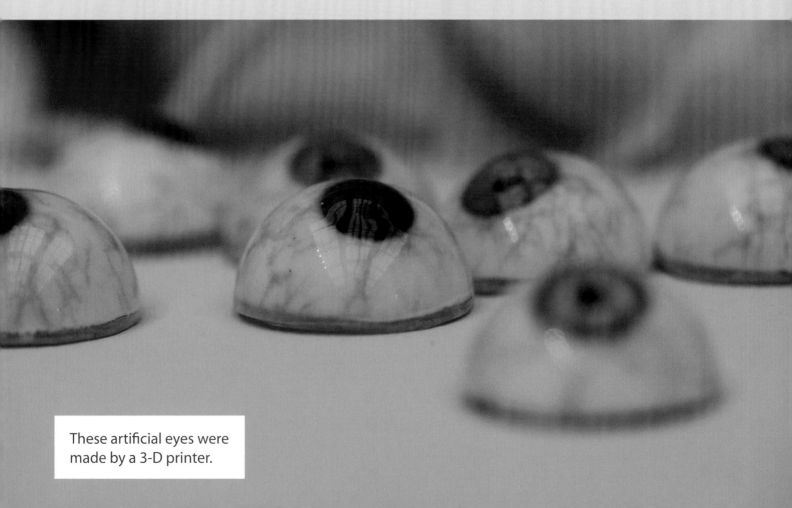

These artificial eyes were made by a 3-D printer.

than a custom-made eye. These eyes are not as close a fit as custom-made eyes, but they may be a solution for thousands of people who would otherwise go without an artificial eye.

## Restoring Vision with Bionic Eyes

Other experts are looking at another issue. Today no type of fake eye can restore normal vision. Someday that may change. Experts are working on bionic eyes that will allow people to see. These eyes would restore vision to people whose optic nerve has not been cut. The optic nerve is cut when a whole eye is surgically removed. So these eyes could help restore vision only in people who have not had an eye removed or who have had only part of an eye removed.

## Organ Transplants

Doctors have been doing organ transplants for many years. The first kidney transplant was in 1950. Other transplants followed. The first liver transplant was in 1963. In 1966 a pancreas was transplanted. A year later the first human heart was transplanted. A lung was transplanted in 1990 and a hand in 1999. In 2010 doctors in France transplanted a whole face. Parts of the eye such as the cornea have been transplanted, but the optic nerve is very complex. Whole eyes have not yet been transplanted.

One type of bionic eye is known as the Argus II. It was made to help blind patients with a disease known as retinitis pigmentosa. It has been approved by the US Food and Drug Administration for use. It restores low levels of vision to blind people. Normal vision is defined as 20/20. This means that a person sees the same line of letters on an eye chart at 20 feet (6.1m) that a normal human eye sees. Legal blindness is defined as 20/200 in the United States. This means a person with vision of 20/200 has to be as close as 20 feet to identify things that people with normal vision can identify from 200 feet (61m). In tests, the best result of vision restoration with the Argus II is about 20/1000. This number means that the patients have some vision restored, but the patients are still

## Retinitis Pigmentosa

The retina has pigment deposits known as "bone spicules."

**DID YOU KNOW?** ❓

**Although humans have five senses, about 70 percent of all sensory perception is through vision.**

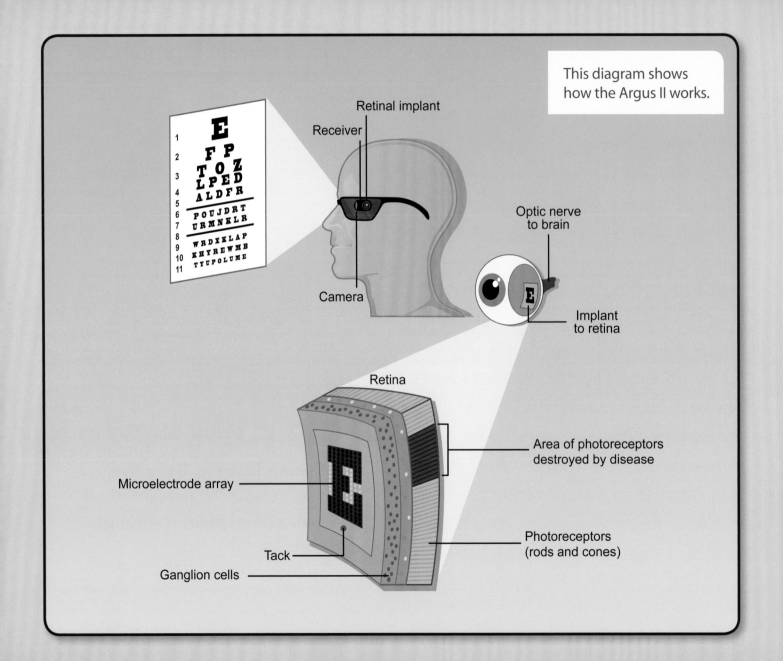

This diagram shows how the Argus II works.

Retinal implant

Receiver

Camera

Optic nerve to brain

Implant to retina

Retina

Area of photoreceptors destroyed by disease

Microelectrode array

Photoreceptors (rods and cones)

Tack

Ganglion cells

legally blind. They can see light and dark, along with some shapes and movements. Having these abilities allow patients to get around more easily.

The Argus II consists of a pair of special glasses. These have a built-in video camera, a visual processor, and a biochip. The biochip is made of 60 electrodes. It is surgically implanted in the patient's retina. The camera captures images. It sends them in the form of light and dark pixels, or tiny dots, to a visual processor that patients wear on their belt. The processor converts the pixels to general electrical patterns. The patterns are wirelessly transmitted to the biochip. This uses the 60 electrodes to send the information up the optic nerve to the brain. This restores the person's ability to detect light, shapes, and movement.

Sheila Nirenberg works at Cornell University in New York. She is developing a different type of bionic eye. It may be able to restore normal vision. It uses electrical patterns or codes to help restore vision. It is based on research on how the retina "talks" to the brain. In a normal eye, if a person sees a cat, a visual signal is sent to the retina. Cells in the retina change the visual signal into a code. This is sent by the optic nerve to the brain.

Nirenberg used lab mice in her research. She put electrodes on the optic nerves of the mice. She showed the mice different images. Then she measured the electric pulses that each image produced. She found that each image created a unique code. She converted each code into a math equation. Then she put the equations on a silicon chip or encoder. She placed the encoder and a tiny camera on glasses. These are worn by the patient. The camera takes in images. The encoder converts each image to a distinct electrical code. The code is then sent to the retina. To make it possible for the code to reach the optic nerve and be sent to the brain, patients are injected in the eye with a special protein. This is a light-sensitive protein. It makes cells in the optic nerve fire and relay the electrical pulses to the brain. The brain then converts the code into the image the camera captured. So far,

Scientists use mice to experiment with Argus II.

# Growing Eyes from Stem Cells

Someday experts may be able to transplant eyes, however, it is not likely that there will be enough eyes to meet the demand. Experts are working on creating eyes from stem cells. Stem cells are able to change into and repair any cell in the body. With this in mind, experts at Tokyo University in Japan took stem cells from frog eggs. They grew the stem cells into partly developed eyes. They then put the eyes into about 60 blind tadpoles. About 25 of these tadpoles could then see. The experts say that with continued study, they can grow human eyes in the future.

Nirenberg's bionic eye has restored near-normal vision to blind mice. It will still be a long time before it can be tested on humans.

The Argus II and Nirenberg's bionic eye could help many people. They cannot help people whose optic nerve has been cut, so experts are working on a new device. It is implanted directly into the vision center of the patient's brain. Such a device is only in the planning stage. If all goes well, it may replace all fake eyes in the future. Fake eyes have come a long way since ancient fake eyes were fastened to cloth and worn over the eyelid. No one knows how fake eyes will change in the future. With the help of modern medical experts, fake eyes will continue to evolve and improve. In fact, it is likely that someday artificial eyes will work as well as real eyes.

# GLOSSARY

**bionic eye (bahy-on-ik ahy):** A visual device designed to restore vision to a blind eye.

**cornea (kawr-nee-uh):** The clear, curved surface in the front of the eye.

**eye socket (ahy sok-it):** The opening in the skull that contains the eye.

**iris (ahy-ris):** The colored part of the eye.

**ocularist (ahk-you-luhr-ist):** A medical technician who makes and fits artificial eyes.

**ocular prosthesis (ahk-you-luhr prahs-thee-sus):** An artificial eye.

**ophthalmologist (of-thuh-mol-uh-just):** A medical doctor who specializes in diseases and defects of the eye.

**optic nerve (op-tik nurv):** A bundle of nerve fibers at the back of the retina that connect the eye and the brain.

**orbital implant (awr-bi-tl im-plant):** A small spherical device that is implanted in the eye socket after the removal of an eye to maintain the shape of the eye socket and provide something for an artificial eye to rest on.

**plaster of Paris (plas-ter uhv par-is):** A quick-setting type of plaster used in making molds and casts.

**pupil (pyoo-puh):** The dark opening in the center of the iris that controls how much light is let into the eye.

**retina (reh-tin-uh):** A nerve layer at the back of the eye that senses light and creates electrical impulses that go through the optic nerve to the brain.

**sclera (skleer-uh):** The white of the eye.

# FOR MORE INFORMATION

## Books

Shannon Caster, *Eyes*. New York: Rosen, 2010. This is a simple book describing how the eye works, with photos and diagrams.

Lois Spilsbury, *Sight*. Chicago: Capstone Press, 2012. This book looks at the science of sight in both humans and animals.

## Websites

**Artificial Eye, How Products Are Made** (www.madehow.com). This article gives a brief history of artificial eyes and describes how artificial eyes are made.

**Artificial Eyes Gallery, College of Optometrists** (www.college-optometrists.org.). This site offers an online "musEYEum" with articles about early artificial eyes, glass eyes, ocular implants, bionic eyes, and more.

**KidsHealth, Your Eyes** (http://kidshealth.org). A site that describes the parts of the eye and how each part works, with lots of interesting facts.

# INDEX

Barbara Sheen is the author of close to 100 books for young people. She lives in New Mexico with her family. In her spare time she likes to swim, walk, garden, and cook.